COMPANY

Clare West

Oxford University Press

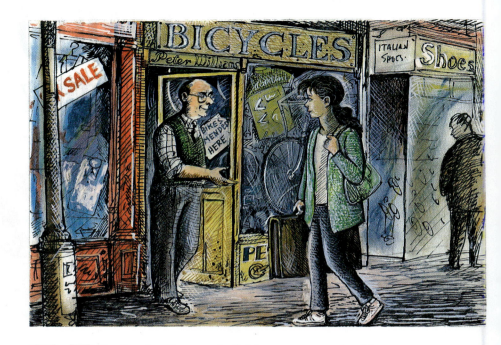

'Hello, Sarah. It's wonderful to see you again. How was your train journey?' asked Uncle Peter.

'Fine, thank you. How are you? And how's business?' answered Sarah. She looked round the kitchen. She remembered it so well from her summer holidays last year, and the year before. There were the old photos of her aunt on the wall, and in a corner she saw several broken bicycles that Uncle Peter was mending.

'Bad, I'm afraid,' said Uncle Peter sadly. ' Not many people are buying bicycles these days. I like mending them but I'm not very good at selling them.'

'Oh dear,' said Sarah. 'I was hoping to work for you in the shop again, like last summer. Now I'm eighteen, I want to learn to drive, so I really need the money for driving lessons.'

'I'm very sorry, my dear,' answered her uncle, 'but why don't we look in the newspaper? I'm sure we can find a summer job for you some-where in Banchester. Look, here are the advertisements for jobs on the back page.'

BANCHESTER EVENING NEWS

JOBS

BOY needed to help in busy camera shop. Phone Banchester 479321

STUDENTS! Do you want to save money for your holidays? Why not work for the Grand Hotel this summer? 20–25 years old only.
Phone Banchester 556623 for an interview.

Banchester General Hospital. Men and women needed for cleaning work. Must be very strong and happy to work hard. Hours of work are 0700–1630, with 30 minutes for lunch, Monday to Friday. The pay is £49.50 a week.

Is your life exciting enough? Come and work for *Cloud Company!* Working for us is never boring! And we pay well! If you want to know more, come to an interview at 11. a.m. on Thursday July 29th, in our first floor office at 24A Edward Street, Banchester.

WORKERS *wanted at Blacks Fruit Factory, near Banchester, on the Starbridge road. No special clothes needed. Good pay, with free lunch in factory restaurant. No students.*

- Which job do you think is the best one for Sarah?

Sarah decided to go to the interview in Edward Street the next day. She found the address, pushed open the door and went upstairs to the first floor.

'Come in,' a man called. There were two men, one sitting behind a desk, and the other one standing near the window.

'Good morning,' she said. 'I've come about the job.'

'Of course,' said the man at the desk, smiling warmly at her. He was tall, with dark hair and a big beard. 'Sit down. I'm Tony.'

'And I'm Frank,' said the other man. He was smiling too.

Sarah sat down in the chair opposite Tony.

'Can you tell me about this job?' she asked.

Tony laughed. 'First, write down your name and address for me, my dear. I think you'll be just right for Cloud Company. Don't you agree, Frank?'

The other man didn't answer. He was looking out of the window. Suddenly, he turned and said quickly to Sarah, 'You'll have to go now. We've got some important business to talk about. You'll hear from Cloud Company soon.'

The two men were looking out of the window as Sarah left the office. They did not see her pick up several pieces of paper from the floor.

Outside, a police car was driving slowly along Edward Street.

Look *at* TONIGHT/THIS WEEK

`tell your wife.`

We know

If you do not

in the Banchester Evening News

to see

pay us

`what you did.`

we will

Here are the instructions:

`£500,000,`

where to bring the money.

• Can you put the pieces of paper together to make a letter?

Every summer, Sarah spent a lot of time with her friend Richard, who lived near Uncle Peter's shop. She immediately went to his house to tell him about her strange interview. He was very interested.

'And look,' she said. 'Look what I found on the floor. I think it's part of a blackmail letter! Read it.'

'This is very exciting!' said Richard. 'I think we should do some detective work. Let's go back to Cloud Company together. There are some questions we should ask those men. And perhaps we can find the other half of the letter, with the instructions.'

But when they went back to 24A Edward Street, they found that there was no name on the door. They pushed open the door, which wasn't locked, and went upstairs to the first floor office. Nobody was there. But they *did* find the clue they were looking for. It was under the desk.

• Can you remember the office when Sarah had her interview there? Find three things which are not there now.

'Several things have gone from the office, you know,' said Sarah, as they sat in the tea-shop in Edward Street, looking at their clues. 'The papers on the desk, the camera, the newspaper, and the map. The man with a beard took his coat with him too, of course. Why do think they left suddenly?'

'I think they're afraid of the police,' answered Richard. 'They saw the police car in the street, asked you to leave, took their things, and ran.'

'It was lucky for us that they left so quickly. I'm sure they didn't want anybody to find these instructions.'

'No, but they weren't hidden, just lying under the desk. I think that the two men forgot to take them. Let's put them with the rest of the blackmail letter. Yes! It's the same letter!'

We know what you did. **If you do not** *pay us* **£500,000, we will** tell your wife. *Here are the instructions:* Look *at* TONIGHT/THIS WEEK **in the Banchester Evening News to see where to bring the money.**

1 Michael Lehmann's film. 1st word
2 Black and white film. 3rd word
3 Odeon Studio One film. 1st word
4 You can see this at the Royal Theatre. 2nd word
5 Black and white film. 3rd word
6 Time of Saturday evening show at the Royal Theatre
7 Newspaper page. 1st word
8 This film won 7 Oscars. 2nd word
9 You can see this at the Little Theatre. 2nd word

'Well,' said Richard, 'I think Cloud Company has sent a letter like this to somebody in Banchester. Perhaps it is somebody we know! Let's see if the newspaper can give us any more clues. Cloud Company said there would be a message on the TONIGHT/THIS WEEK page.'

TONIGHT/THIS WEEK

ABC Studio One
Michael Lehmann's MEET THE APPLEGATES 3.30, 6.15

ABC Studio Two
Winner of 7 Oscars DANCE WITH DEATH 4.20, 7.45

Little Theatre
YOUR MONEY OR YOUR WIFE with Mark King 8.00 Monday to Saturday

Royal Theatre
Sussex Theatre Company in ANIMAL FARM 7.20 Monday to Friday, 2.45 and 8.00 Saturday

Odeon Studio One
Gerard Dépardieu in GREEN WOOD 3.30, 5.50, 8.20

Odeon Studio Two
Trevor Howard in SIR HENRY AT RAWLINSON HOUSE (Black & white) 1.15, 4.25, 7.35

• Can you understand the message, using the instructions on page 8?

'So that's the message!' said Sarah, as she and Richard sat in her uncle's kitchen later that afternoon. 'Where is Green Farm, Richard?'

'It's five miles out of Banchester,' he answered. 'Nobody lives there now. They say that a girl was killed there, a long time ago.'

'There aren't any ghosts at the farm, are there?' asked Sarah, laughing. 'You don't believe in them, do you?'

'Of course not, ' Richard answered crossly, 'but some people *have* seen a ghost in the farmhouse. She wears white and looks very sad.'

'I think perhaps we should go there tonight. What do you think? The Cloud Company men will be there, won't they?'

'Er – perhaps we should go to the police, now,' said Richard.

'I think you're afraid of the ghost at Green Farm!' laughed Sarah. Richard's face did look a little white. 'No, I want to know what job Cloud Company were going to give me, and how many people they are blackmailing. *Then* we can go to the police.'

'All right,' agreed Richard. 'But it might be dangerous. We should arrive at Green Farm early and hide in the fields near the farmhouse.'

'You can have dinner here with me and Uncle Peter,' said Sarah, 'and we'll go after that.'

'Could we borrow two bikes from your uncle?' asked Richard. 'Five miles is a long way to walk.'

'I'm sure that'll be all right,' said Sarah. 'Now what other things do we need to take with us?'

- Look at the things which they could take with them to Green Farm tonight. Which things do you think would be useful?

After dinner that evening, Sarah got everything ready.

'I think I've got everything we need,' she said. 'Let's see: two bikes, a torch, two pencils, some paper, and a map.'

'Where are you going tonight?' asked Uncle Peter.

Sarah looked quickly at Richard. 'Just to Green Farm,' she answered. 'It's such a nice evening for a bike ride.'

'Green Farm?' said Uncle Peter, surprised. 'I knew the people who lived there, you know.'

'Did you?' asked Richard. 'Wasn't a girl murdered there? Did you know her?'

'A girl? You must mean Anne. Anne Atkinson. She was about eighteen when I knew her.'

'When was that, Uncle Peter?' asked Sarah.

'It must be about twenty years ago. She went to work for George Briggs and his wife. They lived at Green Farm then. She cooked and cleaned for them. I remember her well. She was a pretty girl. She often went to visit her boy-friend in London. Then, one day, she left, very suddenly, without telling anybody. I thought she had a better job to go to, or perhaps she wanted to marry her boy-friend.'

'So wasn't a girl murdered at Green Farm?' asked Sarah.

'Oh yes, I'm afraid she was. Look, this is what I read in the newspaper about a year ago. Poor Anne!'

GIRL'S BODY FOUND

This morning the body of an 18-year-old woman was found in the garden at Green Farm. Police think that she was murdered about twenty years ago. Her name was Jane Atkinson, and she worked as a gardener for John Briggs and his wife at Green Farm. People who remember the girl say that she had no friends, and that she spent all her time on the farm. The police are trying to find her murderer.

- Uncle Peter's story is correct but there are some mistakes in the newspaper. Can you find them?

'Well, here we are at Green Farm,' said Richard.

'The house looks very empty,' said Sarah. 'I don't think anybody's lived here for years. Look, the windows are broken! But there's a car in front of the house.'

'We must be careful,' said Richard, speaking quietly. 'If Cloud Company are here, we mustn't let them see us.'

'Shh!' said Sarah suddenly. 'I thought I heard a noise!'

'Perhaps it's the ghost,' said Richard, trying to smile.

'I think it came from the house,' said Sarah slowly. 'Let's go and see! Come on!'

So they walked very quietly up to the house.

'Look!' whispered Richard. 'There they are! In the front room! Are they the men from Cloud Company?'

'Yes! Their names are Tony and Frank,' said Sarah. 'I remember from my interview. What are they doing?'

'They're looking at some papers. If we go a little closer, we'll be able to see what's written on some of them.'

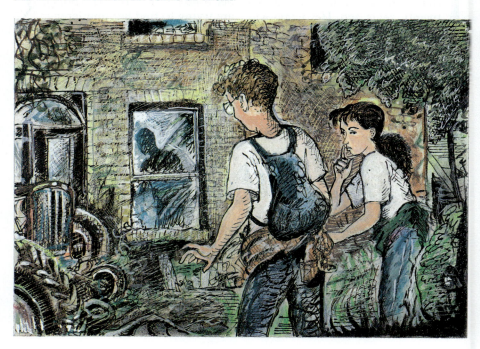

Very carefully Sarah and Richard moved nearer the window. They could see Tony and Frank talking to each other. Tony, the dark man with a beard, was sitting very near the window. He had his arm on a piece of paper, but Sarah and Richard could read some of the words on it. They wrote down the words they could see.

- Can you complete the words on the piece of paper?

'I think we've got the answer, Richard,' said Sarah, looking at the names on their paper.

'They're real criminals! Look how many people they've blackmailed already! Almost one a month!'

'Yes, and it's July now. Do you remember the blackmail letter we found? In it they asked for £500,000, so Mr Harrison must be the person they're waiting for tonight!'

'There's a car coming! It could be him! Quick, let's hide!'

A black Mercedes drove up to the farmhouse, and a big man in a business suit got out. He was carrying a briefcase, and looked very angry.

'That must be Mr Harrison!' Sarah whispered to Richard. 'I think he's got the money in that briefcase.'

'I'm going to go closer to the window to listen to their conversation,' said Richard. 'You stay here.'

Richard watched the man go into the farmhouse, where Tony and Frank met him. They were smiling, but the businessman did not look happy. He opened his briefcase and took out several bags full of twenty-pound notes. Tony and Frank counted them, and then shook hands with him. He went quickly out to his car and drove away very fast.

Richard went back to where Sarah was hiding.

'Well?' she asked. 'What were they saying?'

'I could only hear what the dark man, Tony, said, because Mr Harrison was on the other side of the room.'

• Richard heard Tony's words. Can you write down what the businessman, Mr Harrison said?

'He only brought half the money with him!' said Sarah. 'And he wanted Cloud Company to promise not to tell the police!'

'Do you really think he killed his girl-friend?' asked Richard.

'Well, it's possible. He's ready to pay a lot of money to keep it a secret.'

At that moment, Sarah and Richard saw a white shape coming out of the farmhouse door. It was making a strange sad sound.

'L–l–look, it's the ghost!' screamed Sarah, holding Richard's arm.

Suddenly the ghost started running towards them. There was another dark shape behind it.

'Aha! We've caught you!' shouted a man's voice.

Strong hands held Sarah and Richard, and pulled them towards the house. In the light from the open door, Sarah saw that Tony was holding her. Was it the ghost who was holding Richard? Or was it a man, wearing a white sheet? It was Frank!

'You— you're the ghost!' Sarah cried.

'That's right, my dear,' laughed Frank. 'People stay away from Green Farm because they're afraid of the ghost! That's what we wanted to happen!'

'Lock the boy up in the corner room,' Tony told Frank. 'I'll talk to the girl.' He was smiling coldly. 'Come with me, my dear,' he said to Sarah as he pulled her into the house.

Sarah shouted something to Richard. She used the secret language which they sometimes spoke when they did not want other people to understand.

• Can *you* understand what she said to Richard?

'It's OK, I'll see you soon. They won't hurt us.'

That was Sarah's message to Richard, in their secret language.

Richard sat on the floor near the locked door. The room was very small, and had two windows. Through one window he could see cows in a field and, through the other, the farmyard in front of the farmhouse.

'How can we escape?' he thought. 'Where is Sarah now? I hope Cloud Company don't hurt her.'

Just then he heard a noise outside his door. He listened carefully. He could hear Sarah saying, 'Don't push me!'

Someone opened and closed the door of the room next to his, and he heard Frank say, 'You'll stay in that room for a long time! You and your boy-friend won't be able to tell the police anything!'

PLAN OF GREEN FARM

• Which room is Sarah in now? Which room is Richard in? In which room did Tony and Frank talk to Mr Harrison?

When Sarah was alone in the room, she looked round quickly.

'I must find Richard, and escape!' she thought. 'We must tell the police about Cloud Company!'

But the window in her room was very small, too small for her to get out, and the door was locked.

'Perhaps Richard is in a room near here,' she said to herself. 'I'll knock on the wall and see if he answers.'

She knocked quietly on the wall, hoping that Tony and Frank wouldn't hear her. But nobody answered. So she tried knocking on the wall opposite. Suddenly, she heard someone knocking on the other side of the wall. It must be Richard!

'How can I send him a message?' she asked herself. 'I know! I'll use one knock for A, two knocks for B, and so on.'

She wrote the letters A to Z on her piece of paper, with numbers under them, and counted carefully as she knocked. Then she listened to the message that Richard sent back.

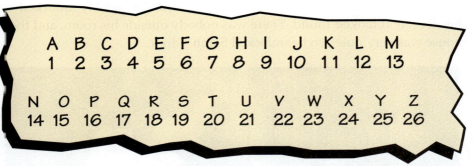

A	B	C	D	E	F	G	H	I	J	K	L	M
1	2	3	4	5	6	7	8	9	10	11	12	13

N	O	P	Q	R	S	T	U	V	W	X	Y	Z
14	15	16	17	18	19	20	21	22	23	24	25	26

• What was Sarah's message to Richard? And what was Richard's answer?

'We must escape!' was Sarah's message.

'I can get the key!' was Richard's answer.

He put a piece of paper under the door. Then he took a pencil from his bag and pushed it into the keyhole. Soon he heard the key fall to the ground on the other side of the door, and he pulled the paper carefully under the door. At last he had the key in his hand. He quickly unlocked his door, and looked round. There was nobody outside his room, and the house was very quiet, so he unlocked Sarah's door.

'Are you all right, Sarah?' he asked. 'They didn't hurt you, did they? What happened? What did Tony say to you?'

'I think he's afraid that we'll go to the police. He says he and Frank are detectives, and that people pay Cloud Company to get information about their husbands or wives or enemies. But I don't believe him. I'm sure they're criminals.'

'Did he explain about the job they advertised?'

'Yes. He says that they wanted some young people to work for them, to find out information about other people, as part of their detective work.'

'But *we* know that they use their information to blackmail people like Mr Harrison! We must leave here and tell the police what we know.'

'Have they gone? I haven't heard any voices for a long time. Let's look in the room they were using, to see if we can find any clues.'

The room was empty, but there was a piece of paper on the table.
'Look!' said Sarah. 'There's only one person who hasn't—'
'Shh!' whispered Richard suddenly. 'Listen!'
Outside they could hear someone walking up to the door of the farm-house.
'It's a man! It's Cloud Company! They've come back,' whispered Sarah. Her face was very white. 'What shall we do?'

• What did Richard say to Sarah, in their secret language?

The door opened and Peter Williams came in.

'Uncle Peter!' shouted Sarah, and put her arms round him. 'I'm so happy to see you! But why have you come?'

'You told me you were going to Green Farm,' said Uncle Peter, smiling. 'I was thinking about it after dinner. And suddenly I thought it could be dangerous here tonight.'

'We've got so much to tell you!' said Sarah.

'I think we should leave here first. Get your bikes, you two, and we'll ride home together. On the way you can tell me what you've found out.'

Sarah and Richard were so excited that they talked without stopping as they all rode home in the dark.

• Look at the map, and find the quickest way home for Sarah, Richard, and Uncle Peter.

'Well, this is all very interesting,' said Uncle Peter, as they sat in his kitchen, drinking coffee. 'So, Cloud Company, that's Tony and Frank, are blackmailers. And Frank pretends to be a ghost, to keep people away from the farm.'

'Why did they lock us up and then leave the farmhouse?' asked Sarah.

'Perhaps they left because they thought that someone was coming,' answered Richard. 'Remember, they left their office in Edward Street when they saw a police car, didn't they?'

'What should we do now?' was Sarah's next question.

'I think we should go to the police,' replied Uncle Peter. 'These men are dangerous. And they know that we know too much about them!'

'I've got an idea,' said Sarah. 'Couldn't we try and catch them? There's one more person they're going to blackmail. What's his name?' She looked at the piece of paper on the table. 'Oh, yes, Stephen Jones. Perhaps they've already sent him his blackmail letter. Why don't we phone him? We could find out when and where he's going to pay Cloud Company the blackmail money. Then the police could wait for Cloud Company and catch them as they take the money.'

'Stephen Jones,' said Uncle Peter quietly. 'I remember him. He was Anne Atkinson's boy-friend, you know, the one who lived in London. I think someone told me he came to live in Banchester a year or two ago. I'd like to see him again. Yes, all right, Sarah, let's phone him. But it's too late to do it tonight. We'll phone him tomorrow.'

Johns, Mrs S.J. 777022
Johnson, Stephen, ... 849713
Johnsons, S.B. 218764
Jones, Sally, ... 704419
Jones, Samuel, ... 623512
Jones, Sandy, ... 513652
Jones, Stephanie, ... 331207
Jones, Stephen, ... 924836
Jones, Steven, ... 557644

- Can you find the right number in the Banchester phone book?

Stephen Jones lived at Box Hill, and his number was 924836. When Uncle Peter phoned him the next day, Stephen asked them all to visit him that evening.

'Yes, you're right about Cloud Company,' he told them. 'They're blackmailing me. They've already asked me to pay them a lot of money. But I can't pay them anything! I'm a maths teacher, and I haven't got much money. They say I killed my girl-friend Anne twenty years ago, and I'm sure that's what the police think too! But I didn't kill her! You must believe me! I moved here from London to try to find out who murdered her. Now I don't know what to do.' He put his head in his hands.

'Stephen,' said Uncle Peter kindly. 'We want to help you. Tell us what really happened to Anne.'

Stephen sat back in his chair and closed his eyes. 'The last time I saw Anne was one weekend when she came to visit me in London. That weekend I thought there was something wrong. She was very quiet and didn't talk much. Just before she went back to Banchester, on the Sunday evening, she started telling me about it. Old George Briggs was very interested in her. Of course, she wasn't interested in *him*. But she was young and pretty, and so Mrs Briggs was jealous. She often shouted at Anne. At Green Farm, Anne sometimes felt ill. She thought perhaps Mrs Briggs was putting something strange in her food. I told her to stay in London with me, because she had no friends in Banchester, but she decided to go back. That was the last time I saw her. And we— we loved each other so much!' Stephen put a hand over his eyes.

GIRL KILLED ON FARM

Police think that Anne Atkinson, aged 18, was killed about twenty years ago by her boy-friend, who was living in London at the time. She worked for Mr and Mrs Briggs at Green Farm. George Briggs said, 'I saw her boy-friend in Banchester at the time she died. I don't think they were happy together.' Mrs Briggs said, 'She had lots of boy-friends in Banchester. Perhaps one of them killed her.' Police are looking for more information, and want to ask people questions about Anne Atkinson's death.

- This is the newspaper story which was in the *Banchester Evening News* a few days after Anne's body was found. Can you find the mistakes in the newspaper?

'We believe you, Mr Jones!' said Sarah and Richard together.

'Now where did Cloud Company ask you to take the money? And when?' asked Uncle Peter.

'Green Farm. Tonight, at 7.30,' answered Stephen. 'But I can't pay them!'

'You won't have to pay them,' said Uncle Peter. 'This is what we'll do. I'll phone the police this afternoon and talk to my friend, Inspector Clark. The police will go to Green Farm tonight, and wait for Cloud Company. You'll go, at 7.30, and *pretend* you've got the money. And we'll be there, to watch the police catch the criminals!'

'That's a wonderful idea!' said Richard and Sarah.

And so, that evening, Uncle Peter, Richard, and Sarah rode their bikes along the quiet road to Green Farm.

'Do you think the police are there?' Sarah asked her uncle.

'I'm sure they'll be there soon,' he answered.

'I feel sorry for the people Cloud Company has blackmailed,' said Richard.

Mr Harrison

Peter Williams

Stephen Jones

Anne Atkinson

Frank

Mr Pettigrew

• Look at the pictures. Can you remember who Cloud Company has blackmailed?

There were police hiding in every corner of the farmyard. Inspector Clark was very pleased to see Uncle Peter again.

'I haven't seen you for years, Peter!' he said. 'Thank you for telling us about Cloud Company. We've been looking for these blackmailers for months. Ah, I think they're coming! Quick, Peter. Hide!'

Everybody was very quiet as Tony and Frank drove into the farmyard. They were talking to each other and didn't see the police. They walked into the house.

'I can hear another car coming!' Sarah whispered to Richard. 'It must be Stephen Jones!'

A very old Mini came round the corner into the farmyard. It stopped in front of the door, and Stephen Jones got out. He was carrying a black briefcase in his hand.

Then everything happened very quickly. As Tony and Frank came out of the house to meet Stephen, policemen jumped out of their hiding places and stopped the two men. A police car arrived in the farmyard. Tony and Frank were pushed into the back of the car and driven away by the police.

'We won't see *them* again for some time!' said the inspector. He turned and shook Stephen's hand. 'Thank you for helping us, Mr Jones,' he said with a smile. 'I must tell you something. The police don't think you killed Anne Atkinson, you know. We now believe that Mrs Briggs killed her, because she was jealous of her. I'm sorry. I know you loved Anne very much.'

Sarah and Richard were talking about Tony and Frank.

'They looked different this time,' said Sarah, and Richard agreed.

• How have Tony and Frank changed?

'Tell me, Peter,' said Stephen, as they sat in Uncle Peter's kitchen drinking coffee. 'Why isn't your bike shop doing well?'

'I'm not very good with money, Stephen,' answered Uncle Peter sadly. 'I never remember how much things cost. Perhaps I should ask people to pay more for my bikes!'

'You know, it's strange,' said Stephen. 'I've always wanted to work in a shop.' He looked round at the broken bicycles in the corner of the kitchen. 'I think I could help you with your business. I'm a maths teacher, remember! I'm very good with numbers. I could leave my job and come here to work for you!'

'That would be wonderful!' said Uncle Peter. 'You could sell the new bikes and I could go on mending old ones! That's what I *really* like doing.'

Stephen turned to Sarah. 'What are you planning to do in Banchester for the rest of the summer?' he asked.

'Well, I wanted to have some driving lessons, but I haven't got enough money, so—'

'Wait a minute! You don't need to learn at a driving school! I can teach you in my car!'

'Really?' said Sarah, a happy smile on her face. 'You'll really teach me to drive? Oh!'

'Of course,' said Stephen.

He turned to the others. 'Look, I want to say thank you to all three of you for helping me. Now I know people don't believe I killed Anne, I can try to forget what happened all those years ago, and start a new life.'

'Tomorrow our story will be in the newspaper,' said Richard. 'Then we'll all be famous! And everybody in Banchester will know about Cloud Company!'

BLACKMAIL IN BANCHESTER

Yesterday the police caught three men at White Farm. 'We think they have black-mailed eight people in Banchester,' Inspector Clark told us. 'They used the name Cloud Company, and a lot of people were afraid of them. We're very pleased we've caught them.'

The police were helped by a brother and sister, Sarah and Richard Williams, who found many of the important clues. Their uncle, Peter Williams, is a teacher in Banchester.

- They all read the newspaper story the next day. Can you find the mistakes in it?

Glossary

advertisement a notice that tells you about jobs, things to sell, etc.

blackmail (n,v) demand money from someone because you have secret information about him/her

briefcase a flat bag to carry papers in

businessman a man who works in an office

clue something that helps to find the answer to a problem or crime

crossly (adv) angrily

farmyard an open place in the middle of farm buildings

gardener a person who works in a garden

ghost a dead person that seems to be alive

interview (n) a meeting when you talk to someone to find out more about him/her

jealous angry or sad feeling about someone

message a piece of information that one person sends to another person

shape (n) form (for example, round or square)

sheet something you put on a bed

towards (prep) in the direction of

useful helpful

whisper (v) talk very quietly

Answers to the puzzles

page 3
The job with Cloud Company

page 5
We know what you did. If you do not pay us £500,000, we will tell your wife. Here are the instructions. Look at TONIGHT/THIS WEEK in the Banchester Evening News to see where to bring the money.

page 7
The camera, the map, the papers, the telephone, the newspaper

page 9
Meet at Green Farm at 8 tonight with money

page 11
The torch, two bicycles, a map, pencils and paper

page 13
Her name was Anne Atkinson. She worked as a cook and cleaner for George Briggs and his wife. She often visited her boy-friend in London.

page 15
J. Stoker stole money. M. Whitehill killed her old mother. J. Hinkley has a girl-friend. J. Pettigrew stole from a shop. P. Masters sold secret plans to another company. M. Harrison killed his girl-friend. S. Jones killed his girl-friend.

page 17
Possible answers:
1 I've (only) brought half the money.
2 It's difficult/a problem to get all the money.
3 But you promise not to tell the police?
4 Please don't tell the police.
5 Yes, I promise I'll pay the rest soon.

page 19
It's OK. I'll see you soon. They won't hurt us.

page 21
Sarah is in the middle room on the right. Richard is in the front room on the right. Tony and Frank were in the front room on the left.

page 23
Sarah's message: We must escape.

Richard's message: I can get the key.

page 25
Stand behind the door. I'll hit him on the head with my torch.

page 27
The bicycle path

page 29
924.836

page 31
She wasn't killed by her boy-friend. Her boy-friend wasn't in Banchester. She was very happy with her boy-friend.

page 33
Mr Harrison, and Mr Pettigrew

page 35
Tony has no beard and he's wearing a hat. Frank has a beard.

page 37
The police caught two men who have blackmailed seven people. Sarah and Richard are not brother and sister. Peter Williams is not a teacher.

Oxford University Press, Great Clarendon Street, Oxford OX2 6DP

Oxford New York
Athens Auckland Bangkok Bogota Bombay
Buenos Aires Calcutta Cape Town Dar es Salaam Delhi
Florence Hong Kong Istanbul Karachi Kuala Lumpur
Madras Madrid Melbourne Mexico City Nairobi
Paris Singapore Taipei Tokyo Toronto

and associated companies in
Berlin Ibadan

OXFORD and OXFORD ENGLISH are trade marks
of Oxford University Press

ISBN 0 19 422479 1

© Oxford University Press 1992

First published 1992
Sixth impression 1997

Cover illustration by Chris Price

Illustrated by Chris Price

Printed in Hong Kong